T0019129

The Third-Year Violoncello Method

by

A.W. BENOY

and

L. BURROWES

NOVELLO PUBLISHING LIMITED

Order No: NOV 916111

The Third-Year Cello Method Order No: NOV 916111

10 lessons covering harmonics on A & D strings, tenor clef, fifth position, sixth position, seventh position, thumb position and treble clef, and higher positions.

ALSO AVAILABLE SEPARATELY

The First-Year Cello Method Order No: NOV 915905

15 lessons covering open strings and first finger notes, first and second finger notes on D & A strings, bowing on successive open strings, first and third finger notes on G, D & A strings, bowing with two notes to the bow, and scales of G, D & C major.

The Second-Year Cello Method Order No: NOV 915969

12 lessons covering crossing strings in key of C major, fourth position in keys of G & C major, half position, first finger extensions backwards in keys of B♭ & F major, forward finger extensions in keys of A & D major, second position, and third position.

Note: To save awkward turnovers, some of the early pieces have had to be contracted by means of Da Capo and Coda signs.

Lesson 1

Harmonic A and D

VARIATIONS CONCERTANTES

© W. Paxton & Co., Ltd. 1969 Assigned to Paxton Music Ltd. 1971

VIOLONCELLO CONCERTO

HAYDN

Lesson 2

Tenor Clef

FRÈRE JACQUES

LLANFAIR

Welsh Hymn Tune

GERMAN DANCE

MOZART

STUCK IM VOLKSTON

SCHUMANN
Op.102, No.1

Lesson 3

Fifth Position

QUARTET, Nº 2

BORODIN

Lesson 4

Sixth Position

SARABANDE

HANDEL

Lesson 5

Sixth Position

LADY FRANCIS NEVILLE'S DELIGHT

Traditional

PLAISIR D'AMOUR

27

Andante tranquillo

G. B. MARTINI

I

II

III

p

p

1st time

p

2nd time

6th position

Fine

cresc.

cresc.

cresc.

D.S. al Fine

Lesson 6

Seventh Position

28

SCALE OF C MAJOR

29

ARPEGGIO OF C MAJOR

30

CAROL TUNE

Con moto

31

mf

dim.

OLD FRENCH MELODY

TCHAIKOWSKY
Op. 39, No. 16

Andante

I
32
II

p
pizz

7th position

arco

ARIOSO

BACH

Adagio
I
33
II
mf
(p)
pizz
tr
mf
cresc.
f
mp
largamente
a tempo
rit.
p a tempo
rit.
p

Lesson 7

Seventh Position

MELODY

RUBINSTEIN

Lesson 8

Thumb Position and Treble Clef

EASTER ALLELUYAH

THE THREE MARYS

MARCH

IRISH FOLK MELODY

Traditional

43

Andante

I

II

III

p

dim.

Lesson 9

Thumb Position

MILITARY SYMPHONY

HAYDN

dim.
p
dim.
p
dim.
p
p
p
1
2

CALLINO CASTUREME

Anon

SONATA IN G MINOR

ECCLES

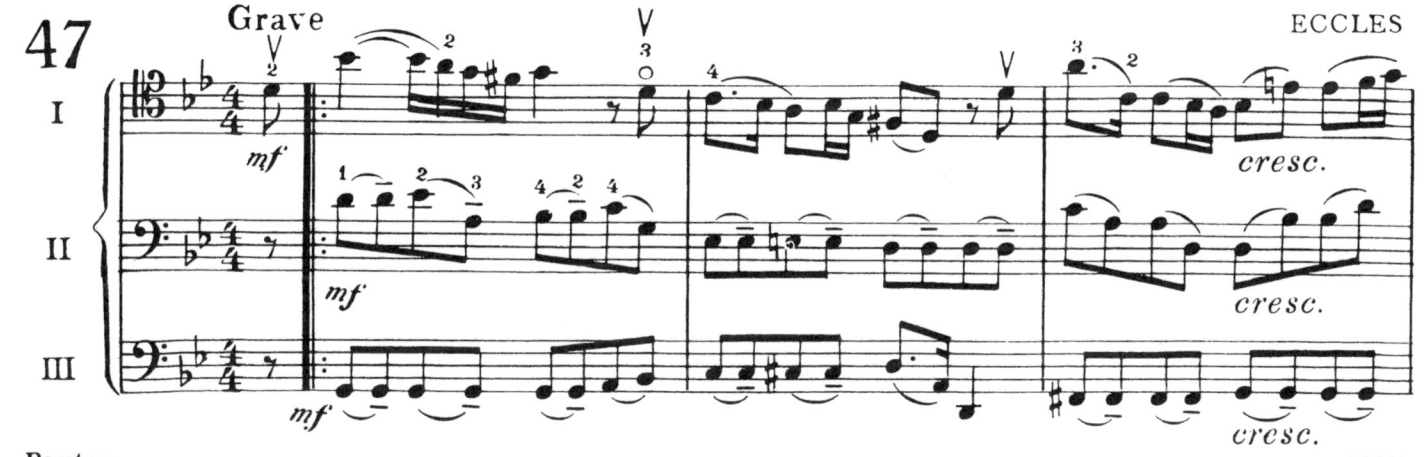

mf
mf
mf
tr
cresc.
f
cresc.
f
cresc.
f

TWENTY ONE EXERCISES FOR VIOLONCELLO, Nº 15

J.L. DUPORT

Lesson 10

Higher Positions

SCALE OF A MAJOR

GERMAN FOLK SONG

VITO

D. POPPER
Op. 54, No. 5

sul A
cresc.
cresc.
cresc.
f
f
f
1
2
mf
mf
mf
f
mf
p
f
ff
mf
p
f
ff
mf
p

STUDY

J. J. F. DOTZAUER

f
cresc.
dim.
D String
p
mf